SUCCESSFUL STAFFING IN A DIVERSE WORKPLACE

A Practical Guide To
Building An Effective And Diverse Staff

Maureen C. Orey

Richard Chang Associates, Inc.
Publications Division
Irvine, California

SUCCESSFUL STAFFING IN A DIVERSE WORKPLACE

A Practical Guide To Building An Effective And Diverse Staff

Maureen C. Orey

Library of Congress Catalog Card Number
95-83809

© 1996, Richard Chang Associates, Inc.
Printed in the United States of America

ISBN 1-883553-67-9

Richard Chang Associates, Inc.
Publications Division
41 Corporate Park, Suite 230
Irvine, CA 92714
(800) 756-8096 • Fax (714) 756-0853

RICHARD CHANG ASSOCIATES

ACKNOWLEDGMENTS

About The Author

Maureen C. Orey is an experienced consultant, trainer, and recruiter. She specializes in training, staffing, and human resources, particularly in relation to disability and diversity issues. She is well known for her ability to assist human resource professionals in developing their comfort zone when interacting with people with disabilities.

The author would like to acknowledge the support of the entire team of professionals at Richard Chang Associates, Inc. for their contribution to the guidebook development process. In addition, special thanks are extended to the many client organizations who have helped to shape the practical ideas and proven methods shared in this guidebook.

Additional Credits

Editor: Sarah Ortlieb Fraser

Reviewer: Keith Kelly

Graphic Layout: Christina Slater

Cover Design: John Odam Design Associates

PREFACE

The 1990's have already presented individuals and organizations with some very difficult challenges to face and overcome. So who will have the advantage as we move toward the year 2000 and beyond?

The advantage will belong to those with a commitment to continuous learning. Whether on an individual basis or as an entire organization, one key ingredient to building a continuous learning environment is *The Practical Guidebook Collection* brought to you by the Publications Division of Richard Chang Associates, Inc.

After understanding the future *"learning needs"* expressed by our clients and other potential customers, we are pleased to publish *The Practical Guidebook Collection*. These guidebooks are designed to provide you with proven, *"real-world"* tips, tools, and techniques— on a wide range of subjects—that you can apply in the workplace and/or on a personal level immediately.

Once you've had a chance to benefit from *The Practical Guidebook Collection*, please share your feedback with us. We've included a brief *Evaluation and Feedback Form* at the end of the guidebook that you can fax to us at (714) 756-0853.

With your feedback, we can continuously improve the resources we are providing through the Publications Division of Richard Chang Associates, Inc.

Wishing you successful reading,

Richard Y. Chang
President and CEO
Richard Chang Associates, Inc.

TABLE OF CONTENTS

"The human mind, when stretched by a new idea, never regains its original dimension"

Oliver Wendell Holmes

CHAPTER ONE

INTRODUCTION

Diversity, like change, is here to stay. The dynamics of a diverse workplace are sometimes difficult to define. Diversity is more than affirmative action. It is not simply having different populations represented within your organization, it is the effective comingling of these populations working together to achieve the same goal. The implications of true diversity present a unique challenge to management today; not only to recruit and hire a diverse population, but to also provide an environment to retain this diversity.

Why Read This Guidebook?

If you have a role to play in staffing decisions for your team, your department, or your organization, *Successful Staffing In A Diverse Workplace* will provide you with the structure to put an effective staffing model and process into action. It will also educate you about the benefits of diversity.

Successful Staffing In A Diverse Workplace will help you look at diversity from more than an administrative perspective. It will challenge you to reconsider your definition of diversity, and then help you prepare to manage a truly diverse workplace.

Finally, this guidebook will present you with some basic information about communication and etiquette in reference to various cultures and disabilities at work and in society.

Who Should Read This Guidebook?

Successful Staffing In A Diverse Workplace is designed to assist managers, supervisors and human resource professionals in preparing for, selecting, and retaining a more diverse work force. The concepts of the Diversity Staffing Model™ are intended for use not only with external recruitment, but also for internal staffing decisions, such as the selection of team members, project groups and committees.

Any manager or supervisor who routinely hires professional, technical and non-exempt employees should read this guidebook. Human resource professionals should also use this guidebook to establish a consistent approach to staffing for a diverse workplace. Businesses of all sizes, as well as not-for-profit organizations can benefit from utilizing the Diversity Staffing Model.

When And How To Use It

Use this guidebook when you are seeking to increase your staff size, or after you have committed to increasing your company's diversity. When staffing decisions are made on a group basis, make sure your colleagues have a chance to cover the highlights of the guidebook too. This guidebook can be a resource for you as you continue to grow and develop. You can revisit your staffing approach, as well as your success with retaining a diverse work force.

You can utilize the resources in this guidebook on many different levels. You may be a human resources professional responding to a company-wide diversity program, a new human resources professional, or a manager, supervisor, or team leader with additional staffing responsibilities. You can also use the guidebook as a support tool when training managers on the Diversity Staffing Model.

For further reading and training application material on the topic of workplace diversity, please see the entire Workplace Diversity Series of guidebooks (*five titles*) of which this guidebook is a part. The lead or *"parent"* guidebook in the series, *Capitalizing On Workplace Diversity*, presents an overall approach and model for an organization or work group to succeed with diversity as one of its core strengths.

One element of this overall model, building work force capability, is expanded upon in detail in the three other guidebooks in the series, *Successful Staffing In A Diverse Workplace, Team Building For Diverse Work Groups*, and *Communicating In A Diverse Workplace*. Each of these guidebooks presents a platform from which employees can improve their skills and further develop the competencies needed to contribute to the success of a diverse organization.

The Organizational Diversity Success Model™

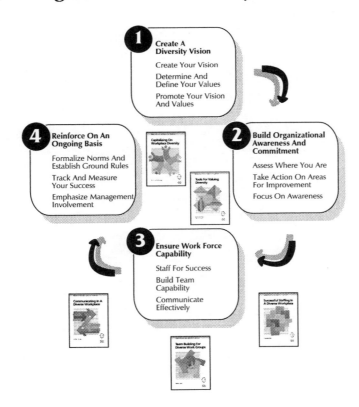

1 Create A Diversity Vision

Create Your Vision

Determine And Define Your Values

Promote Your Vision And Values

2 Build Organizational Awareness And Commitment

Assess Where You Are

Take Action On Areas For Improvement

Focus On Awareness

3 Ensure Work Force Capability

Staff For Success

Build Team Capability

Communicate Effectively

4 Reinforce On An Ongoing Basis

Formalize Norms And Establish Ground Rules

Track And Measure Your Success

Emphasize Management Involvement

THE IMPACT OF DIVERSITY ON STAFFING

*"Just because we are equal . . .
does not mean we are the same."*
Anonymous

What Is Diversity?

Diversity can best be defined in terms of differences among individuals in a work group, such as:

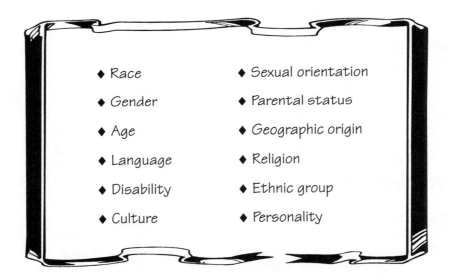

- ◆ Race
- ◆ Gender
- ◆ Age
- ◆ Language
- ◆ Disability
- ◆ Culture
- ◆ Sexual orientation
- ◆ Parental status
- ◆ Geographic origin
- ◆ Religion
- ◆ Ethnic group
- ◆ Personality

and *any* difference that is irrelevant to one's success in the organization.

One of the major areas of difficulty in dealing with diversity is how people react to differences. In most cases, peoples' responses have already been imprinted since early childhood, based on a wide range of influences.

When individuals start to realize the extent to which these influences have shaped their perceptions, awareness begins. Awareness then leads to greater understanding and ultimately, the potential to build a positive environment. Awareness also opens a window of opportunity for you and your organization to focus on a new direction!

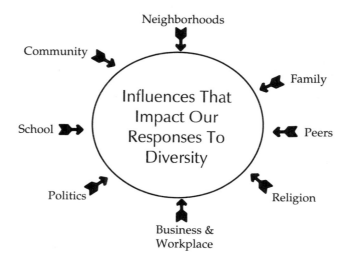

Workplace Demographics

Today's workplace is an ever-changing environment. As we grow and develop, we continue to diversify, and we continue to define diversity in new and more specific terms. We are all different in very fundamental ways; our differences are manifested through our personalities, physical abilities, genders, ages, religious beliefs, races, cultures or many other unique attributes. The challenge for the managers of today's workplace is to harness the strength of this diversity, to nurture it and mold it into the productive workplace we need and desire.

The aspects of diversity that present the most significant challenge in the workplace are cultural differences, language, communication styles and differences in physical ability.

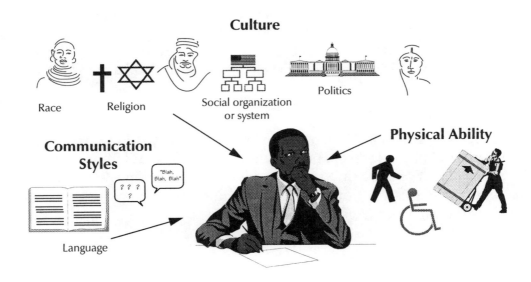

DIVERSITY CHALLENGES

Cultural Differences

Webster's New Collegiate Dictionary defines culture as *"the customary beliefs, social forms, and material traits of a racial, religious, or social group."* Culture is how we identify who we are and who is different from us, and it is developed through our belief systems. These belief systems affect our values, attitudes, etiquette, motivation, family structure, as well as our work ethic. Our upbringing, environment and surroundings influence who we are and how we react to various situations. This difference in belief systems is where conflict arises. As a manager of a diverse work force, you cannot discount the impact of the differences in cultural values on the work environment. Sensitivity to cultural differences is an important part of understanding the perspectives of the employees you are managing.

Language

 An American college student was assigned a dormitory room with a young Englishman. His father asked him how he liked rooming with the Englishman. *"Except for the one standing argument,"* said the student, *"it's fine." "What's the argument?"* asked the father. *"Each of us accuses the other of having an accent,"* the student replied.

There are more than 150 languages spoken in the world today. The idioms of language create both obvious and subtle differences in communication. The first step to open communication is self-awareness. Beware of your own style of communication, including your biases toward language and cultural issues.

Communication Styles

 Communication styles are not only influenced by language and accent, but also by cultural attitudes toward authority, gender, and personal disclosure. Many miscommunications occur as a result of one person speaking with incomplete or unclear information to someone of another culture. Sometimes the differences can be as simple yet difficult as adult/child communication, as is shown in this anecdote:

"Where do I come from?" the little girl asked her mother. The mother launched a long explanation of the birds and the bees. *"No,"* said the child impatiently. *"My friend comes from Boston. Where do I come from?"*

Physical Ability

People with disabilities are included in the most recent civil rights movement. It is estimated that 65 to 70 percent of all adult persons with disabilities who are able to work are unemployed. It is not due to their lack of ability, but due to the lack of opportunity made available to them. Many employers assume that it is very expensive to hire and accommodate a person with a disability, however the fact is that most accommodations cost only a few hundred dollars.

There are many different kinds of disabilities, both obvious physical challenges, as well as hidden physical or psychological challenges. As with the variances and dynamics brought to the work force by different ethnic groups, people with disabilities also add a unique dimension to the workplace; they enrich us and challenge us to sometimes revisit the *"standard operating procedures"* of how and why we do the things we do.

Other Differences

Work force diversity is about inclusion, regardless of our differences. Although the focus is often on the more obvious differences, such as culture, language, and physical ability; other differences also bring strength, ideas, and creativity to a work group. These include differences in age, gender, religious beliefs, sexual orientation, place of origin and so on.

Valuing Differences

A recent study concluded that a diverse work force is a more effective and productive work force. There are many benefits to the diversity of your workplace. Each workplace comes complete with different cultural, economic and familial approaches to problem solving and communication, as well as unique perspectives on ethics, authority and business.

The most common benefits that stem from a diverse work force include:

- an improved work force quality

- increased market sensitivity

- and organizational flexibility

The study emphasized that a diverse workplace is inevitable, but the benefits of diversity are not. The environment within an organization will determine if the benefits of diversity are realized. Specific steps must be taken to create an environment where all personnel feel welcome and valued for what they bring to the organization.

The statistical demographics of today's workplace will change from region to region, and occupation to occupation. The only constant is that we continue to develop and change through the individual contributions of a vast combination of cultures, languages and abilities all working together to achieve success in today's workplace. This guidebook will help you to create a diversity friendly environment through the systematic approach of The Diversity Staffing Model, for successful staffing in a diverse workplace.

CHAPTER TWO WORKSHEET: DIVERSITY AND YOUR APPROACH TO STAFFING

1. How would you describe the diverse make-up of your work group or your organization?

Cultural: _____

_____

Gender: _____

_____

Ability:_____

_____

Language: _____

_____

Age: _____

_____

Religion:_____

_____

Other:_____

_____

_____

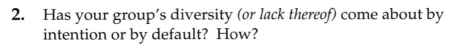
2. Has your group's diversity *(or lack thereof)* come about by intention or by default? How?

Intentional efforts: _____

_____

_____

_____

_____

_____

_____

Diversity by default: _____

_____

_____

_____

_____

_____

_____

_____

_____

3. What benefits has your work group experienced from its diverse make-up? What additional benefits would you like to see?

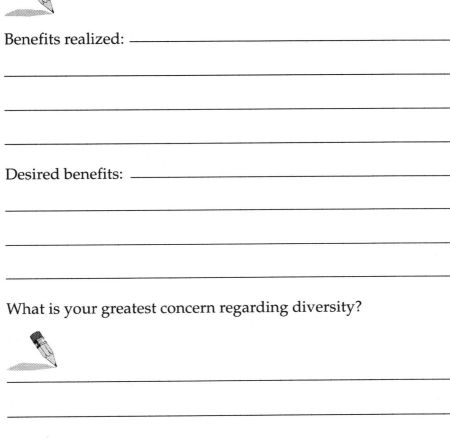

Benefits realized: _____

_____

_____

_____

Desired benefits: _____

_____

_____

_____

4. What is your greatest concern regarding diversity?

_____

_____

_____

_____

_____

_____

_____

_____

STRATEGIES FOR
SUCCESSFUL STAFFING

Diversity Staffing Model

The Diversity Staffing Model™ is a five-phase approach to successful staffing in a diverse workplace. By following this approach, you can create an environment that will help you realize the benefits of diversity.

Each phase of the staffing model brings you closer to building and retaining a diverse workplace. Keep in mind however, that each hiring department or team may experience varying levels of success, as they deal with the challenges of capitalizing on diversity. For best results, your organization's commitment to diversity must be unwavering.

Focus your direction

Recruit for success

Retain and maintain your diversity

DIVERSITY STAFFING MODEL™

Orient and train your team

Select the best

Phase One: Focus Your Direction

Focus is the process of assessment, strategic planning and goal setting to determine the direction and vision of your organization. Part of this process requires identifying the most important issues within your organization. In this case, let's assume that diversity has been identified as a key priority. Now that you have identified diversity as a priority, you must define your vision and goals for how you plan to address this issue within your organization. Next you must develop an organizational commitment to diversity and put into place a plan of action. It is important to communicate your commitment to both internal and external customers, so that all levels of personnel, contractors and customers know your commitment.

Once all the pieces are in place, you can work on building an environment of empowerment. Empowerment means enabling each employee to accept their role in the process of building a more diverse work force. Every employee must act responsibly and take action to implement the organizational commitment to diversity.

The steps you must take during the *"Focus"* phase include; Assess, Plan, Commit, Communicate, and Empower.

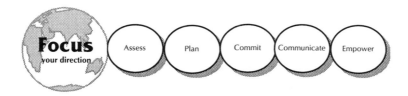

Each step builds on another, and in order to reach the stage of empowerment effectively, it is important to build a solid foundation of assessment, planning, goal setting and communication.

Phase Two: Recruit For Success

Recruit means to seek out and build your staff with a vision for diversity. The Diversity Staffing Model approach includes recruiting both internally and externally. When staffing for diversity, the following concepts should be considered *(although not limited to):*

Internal Recruiting

◆ Promotions
◆ Transfers
◆ Work Teams
◆ Committees
◆ Project Groups

External Recruiting

◆ Networking
◆ Community Organizations
◆ Friends & Family
◆ Colleges & Universities
◆ Professional Associations

Always keep in mind the balance and make-up of each work group or setting. Strive for diversity at all levels in order to maintain the integrity of your organization's commitment to diversity.

Phase Three: Select The Best

Selection is the process of choosing the best candidate for an available position. This does not necessarily mean that the position is being filled from the outside. Position here can be defined as an opening on a committee, work team, etc.

An organization that emphasizes diversity needs to include a *"comprehensive"* interview and selection process. Accurate job descriptions play an important role, as do structured and consistent interviewing techniques.

Here are the essential steps of the interview process and the approximate time you should devote to each step:

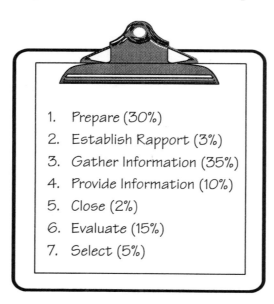

1. Prepare (30%)
2. Establish Rapport (3%)
3. Gather Information (35%)
4. Provide Information (10%)
5. Close (2%)
6. Evaluate (15%)
7. Select (5%)

Communication and etiquette issues arise when dealing with individuals who are different from us, such as those who come from a different cultural background, and also those who may have a visible or hidden disability. The situation can be confusing and intimidating, but the key concept to remember as an interviewer is: accept each person as a viable candidate, then discuss the essential functions of the job in a non-biased manner.

Phase Four: Orient And Train Your Team

The aim of orientation and training is to help make a smooth, positive adjustment to the workplace. To do this you will need a well-planned and executed orientation program that will:

- ◆ Reduce the employee's anxiety level
- ◆ Foster a positive attitude toward the organization
- ◆ Reinforce or establish realistic job expectations
- ◆ Communicate how diversity is incorporated into the norms and values of the organization, along with examples
- ◆ Communicate how diversity ties into the organization's overall vision and goals

The goal of training, whether for new or existing employees, is to continually improve the match between the requirements of the job and the skills and competencies of the employees.

When working with individuals from diverse backgrounds, it is important to consider not only differences in communication, but also differences in learning styles due to cultural or disability issues. It may be necessary to accommodate a disability within the training environment. For example, a deaf individual may need an interpreter, or a person with a learning disability may need extended training and/or testing time.

To be effective in the orientation and training process, it is essential that you remember the different modalities in which people learn:

♦ Visual: Means that a person learns more effectively through what they see.

♦ Auditory: Means that a person learns and processes information through what they hear.

♦ Kinesthetic: A kinesthetic learner works more effectively by doing what it is they are trying to learn.

Truly effective training will incorporate all approaches to learning in order to maximize the retention rate of the learner.

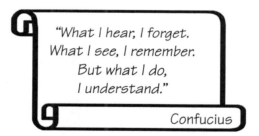

"What I hear, I forget.
What I see, I remember.
But what I do,
I understand."

Confucius

Phase Five: Retain And Maintain Your Diversity

The real key to successful staffing in a diverse workplace is the ability to retain the work force that is in place. Additionally, keep in mind that making a commitment to diversity means more than striving for immediate results such as improved demographics within your organization. Simply recruiting for diversity will not necessarily mean that those whom you employ will stay with your organization if they do not feel welcome or supported. Training programs geared toward heightening the awareness level and appreciation for diversity can be helpful to educate employees as your organization enforces its commitment to diversity. However, training and development can not be a stand-alone activity.

There must be additional support systems in place such as :

- ◆ Support groups
- ◆ Career development
- ◆ Job sharing
- ◆ Child care alternatives
- ◆ Flexible work schedules

These options will enable people from a variety of backgrounds and abilities to be more productive and committed to your organization.

Supervising a Diverse Work Force

It is often taken for granted that clear communication and feedback will occur between employees and supervisors. What is not considered however, is the difference in communication styles between cultures and genders. Differences also occur with attitudes toward authority. In many cultures, for example:

- ◆ Age is to be respected
- ◆ Males are often found in positions of authority
- ◆ Employees should not question authority
- ◆ Workers do not act without direct orders from their superior

Excellent communication skills are not inherited, they are learned and they require constant reevaluation and revision. Effective managers and team members learn to identify the different communication styles of others they work with, and how to adapt their communication approaches.

Case Example: Theme Park USA

To get a clearer picture of how the Staffing Model works, let's take a look at a theme park struggling with the impact of diversity.

Theme Park USA...

is an internationally known and recognized family entertainment organization. Recently, the park conducted an employee satisfaction survey and the results showed that employees were concerned with the organization's responsiveness to their needs. It seemed that although the organization did an excellent job serving a diverse clientele, it did not effectively address the needs of the diverse work force employed at the park.

In response to these issues, Shane, the President of Theme Park USA, created a task force of select managers from different areas of the park to look at the dynamics of the situation. Rochelle, the Director of Human Resources, and Mike, the Training Coordinator for Park Operations, were selected to lead the task force. They gathered additional information through employee surveys and focus groups. The task force evaluated the feedback and developed a plan of action to address the issues. They saw a need to have a comprehensive approach to resolve the employee concerns. They chose to follow the Diversity Staffing Model to develop their action plan.

CHAPTER THREE WORKSHEET:
YOUR STAFFING STRATEGY

1. What are your work group/organization's strengths and areas for improvement in each of the phases of the Diversity Staffing Model?

   a. Focus your direction:

Strengths	Areas For Improvement
_____	_____
_____	_____
_____	_____
_____	_____
_____	_____

   b. Recruit for success:

Strengths	Areas For Improvement
_____	_____
_____	_____
_____	_____
_____	_____
_____	_____

c. Select the best:

Strengths	Areas For Improvement
_____	_____
_____	_____
_____	_____
_____	_____
_____	_____

d. Orient and train your team:

Strengths	Areas For Improvement
_____	_____
_____	_____
_____	_____
_____	_____
_____	_____

e. Retain and maintain your diversity:

Strengths	Areas For Improvement
_____	_____
_____	_____
_____	_____
_____	_____
_____	_____

2. Which of the areas for improvement identified in Question # 1 are your most pressing concerns?

_____

_____

_____

_____

_____

_____

3. What are the underlying issues behind these areas of concern?

_____

_____

_____

_____

_____

_____

_____

_____

PHASE ONE: FOCUS YOUR DIRECTION

Focus provides you with a framework for determining the direction your work group or organization will follow. This phase involves assessment, strategic planning, and goal setting to identify the steps to develop and achieve your vision as an organization.

One of the key issues in this phase is obtaining direct support from management personnel. It has been proven that diversity programs with strong upper management support are more effective and achieve lasting results.

Let's look at the key elements of developing and communicating your group's focus on successful staffing in a diverse workplace.

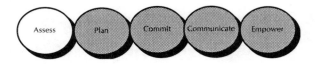

Assess

Your staff or team members are the best source of information about your organization's current approach to diversity. There are a variety of ways to gather and compile this information:

- ◆ Suggestion Boxes
- ◆ Employee Surveys
- ◆ Focus Groups
- ◆ Task Forces
- ◆ Brainstorming Sessions

Once the information and feedback are gathered and summarized, develop your strategy and set specific goals. Additionally, an important part of the assessment phase is to have all key personnel do an evaluation of their preparation for a renewed commitment to diversity. The Diversity Staffing Assessment Worksheet *(please see the Appendix for a sample copy)* is an effective tool to utilize for this process.

Once the task force and focus groups. . .

at Theme Park USA identified diversity as the focal point, they set out to clarify the issues and set goals for the organization.

The task force chose to do a follow-up employee survey to specifically assess the concerns regarding diversity. Their goal was to identify the most significant concerns and develop feasible solutions. They came up with the following goals as a result of the survey results. These would be known as the Diversity Initiatives:

DIVERSITY INITIATIVES

Goal #1 - Increase recruitment for diversity

Goal #2 - Improve the selection and promotion processes

Goal #3 - Implement a diversity training program

Goal #4 - Shift our environment toward embracing diversity as an organizational strength

Plan

Before you can take action on your goals, they need to be clearly defined. The most effective way to define your organizational goals is to write out a sentence or two explaining each goal. Then, specific action items should be written in clear and measurable terms.

Shane, the President, believed . . .

that in order to have a consistent approach, it was important to define their goals in more specific terms. The task force spent time brainstorming ideas to align the stated goals for diversity with specific action items, and initiate movement toward meeting their goals.

The defined goals and action plans for the Diversity Initiatives of Theme Park USA are both specific and measurable.

Goal #1—Increase recruitment for diversity

We will expand our recruiting program to reach out to untapped resources. Our goal is to increase the diverse applicant pool, resulting in a more diverse population of new employees.

Action items or *"How to"*:

♦ Attend more career fairs at high schools and colleges

♦ Revise brochures to reflect diverse populations

♦ Ensure that all recruiters for the organization are sensitive to diversity issues and encourage all diverse applicants to apply

♦ Reach out to other community organizations to set up mini job fairs at their locations

Goal #2—Improve selection and promotion processes

We will revisit all current hiring and promotion practices, especially with individual hiring managers, ensuring that there are no discriminatory activities.

Action items or *"How to"*:

♦ Assess the current balance of diversity in the workplace

♦ Target and develop individuals for future promotions

♦ Evaluate all interview questions for cultural/diversity biases

Goal #3—Implement a diversity training program

We will incorporate the concepts of valuing diversity into all new employee orientation and ongoing training done at Theme Park USA. This will include two perspectives—customer diversity and co-worker diversity. Additionally, we will develop a comprehensive program for all management personnel.

Action items or *"How to"*:
- Human Resources staff and all managers will be the first to attend company-wide diversity training program
- Blend the concepts of diversity into all management training
- Incorporate diversity philosophies into new employee orientations

Goal #4—Shift our environment toward embracing diversity as an organization strength

Without a positive and supportive environment, a diverse population may not be a retained population. This is as important for diverse workers as it is for front-line personnel and management staff. Our goal is to evaluate the needs of various populations to identify what environmental changes would be feasible and rewarding for both our organization and our employees.

Action items or *"How to"*:
- Support groups
- Career development
- Job sharing
- Child care alternatives
- Flexible work schedules

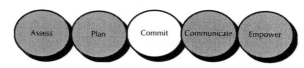

Commit

Once you have identified your vision and defined your goals for diversity, you must develop and incorporate an organizational commitment to diversity. Your organizational commitment should define and clearly communicate the values you have assigned to this issue.

Shane understood . . .

the importance of taking a positive stance on diversity. He personally played an integral part in defining the values and forming the organization's commitment to diversity.

Theme Park USA's commitment to diversity is as follows:

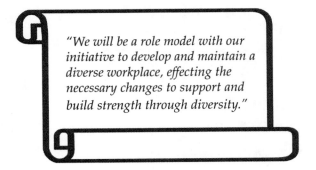

"We will be a role model with our initiative to develop and maintain a diverse workplace, effecting the necessary changes to support and build strength through diversity."

Communicate

The next step is to communicate your vision to both internal and external customers. Develop a marketing plan to approach this strategically. A marketing plan should incorporate the three "T's."

Time lines: Develop appropriate time-oriented goals for your marketing campaign. Consider the steps involved, and their duration.

Targets: Know the markets you intend to pursue. Remember, there is a multitude of resources and organizations to partner with and utilize within each community.

Techniques: Be aware of cultural communication differences when developing your specific marketing strategies. Many organizations have been embarrassed as a result of cultural miscommunications!

Internal marketing

When marketing a concept internally, consider using the following resources:

- ◆ Employee newsletters & information bulletins

- ◆ Posters & banners

- ◆ Employee referral incentive programs

- ◆ Specific training programs

Shane realized . . .

that all levels of personnel must have a heightened awareness of diversity issues. To begin the process of communicating the commitment to diversity, he determined that they would carry out a marketing plan in two phases, internal and external.

The internal marketing campaign would include two components: publications and programs.

Publications

To kick off the internal marketing campaign, a park-wide contest would be held to develop a logo to represent the Diversity Initiatives. The person who submitted the winning logo would receive an extra day off with pay! The goal now is to saturate the following resources with the Diversity Initiatives and the corresponding programs to support the commitment using employee newsletters, information bulletins, posters in each work area, banners and bulletin boards.

Programs

Another kick-off event for Theme Park USA would be managed by Rochelle in Human Resources. The number of new employee referrals coming from existing employees had always been steady and consistent, and had provided a good base of knowledgeable applicants. To increase the utilization of this resource, a friends & family *"Pick a Winner"* hiring incentive program was developed. Each existing employee who referred someone who gets hired, would receive $25.00 initially. The referring employee would receive another $25.00 after their friend had been employed for 90 days.

Rochelle explained to her assistant Jose, that there was another source at their fingertips in which to tap for diversity—the population of current employees with promotional potential. She reminded him that one of the Diversity Initiatives was to develop individuals for promotional opportunities. In conjunction with the kick-off for the *"Pick a Winner"* program, they decided it would be a good idea to remind all current employees about the channels for self-improvement and career development. They made posters to spotlight the benefits.

Grow With Us

Career Development Opportunities
with Theme Park USA!

♦ Learn what it takes to do another job through the job
shadowing program.

♦ Ask the *"expert"*—find a mentor to learn from by participating in a mentor partnership with a theme park veteran.

♦ Let us help you advance yourself with continuing education.
Ask about reimbursed tuition through our Educational
Assistance Program.

♦ Are you interested in other advanced training programs?
Bring us the info about it, and we will do what we can to
support you.

External marketing

The approach for external marketing will be different of course. The types of resources to consider here would be:

- Community activities & organizations
- Brochures & commercials
- "Awareness" days within your organization
- Language-friendly products & services

In response to the need to communicate...

their commitment to diversity to the public as well, the task force of Theme Park USA suggested that the corporate marketing team take on this project. The goal in marketing would be that Theme Park USA would become a role model for empowering diversity in their organization.

The marketing team identified two components to develop in conjunction with their external marketing plan:

1) Community Outreach
In order to communicate their commitment to diversity, Theme Park USA wanted to be fully immersed within the community. They began sending representatives to various community activities and organizations. They advertised volunteer opportunities to their employees, participated in fund-raisers, community clean-up campaigns and local parades.

"Awareness" days at the park were held to increase the exposure of their Diversity Initiatives. The goal for these events was to offer a discounted admission rate to various diverse community groups and increase partner-ships. Another goal was to provide employees with an opportunity to experience first-hand working with a targeted, diverse customer base.

2) Products & Services
The Public Relations and Marketing Departments worked together to update all company brochures and advertising campaigns to include the diversity logo and company initiatives. Additionally, they began developing language-friendly products and services. These products and services included having anything ranging from brochures, park maps, restaurant menus and informa-tion assistance available in as many languages as possible....

Empower

A key point in the focus process is to empower employees and then allow the process to happen. Empowerment means *"to give authority."* When considering diversity, empowerment is giving each employee the authority to act in support of your organizational commitment. To make empowerment truly effective, you must first provide employees with the appropriate tools of knowledge so they can act responsibly. Next, you must be supportive of new ideas, and be willing to accept the decisions being made.

Be prepared for setbacks as people begin to test the waters and act on their own. There is a learning curve to be considered for both the employee and organization as the boundaries of responsibility are defined. However, usually an employee who is empowered and given the freedom to act responsibly will accept the responsibility and is likely to increase their effectiveness, and have higher productivity and increased job satisfaction.

The task force was committed. . .

to realizing the organizational goals for diversity. They believed in involving all employees in the process to be successful. They had learned that an involved employee is a retained employee. The process of empowerment would allow each and every employee at all levels within the organization to take part in achieving the established goals.

The next step was to develop an ongoing diversity team to monitor and maintain the effectiveness of the Diversity Initiatives. This team would be open to any employee who, with the approval of their supervisor, chose to get involved and support the organizational commitment to diversity.

One of the Diversity Initiatives was to develop a company-wide diversity training program. Mike, the Training Coordinator for Park Operations, evaluated the survey results to identify areas of concern regarding diversity. He also met with Rochelle and the task force to brainstorm different strategies for empowering employees. They created a list of *"Tools for Empowering Employees"* that could be given to managers. Mike used this list to develop new training modules and incorporate them into a new employee orientation program.

Tools for Empowering Employees

1. Educate & inform all employees regularly!

2. Develop a communication board system within each facility or worksite to ensure that all employees get all messages.

3. Reward employees who take the initiative to correct a problem, or smooth a conflict (customer or co-worker).

4. Don't assume that an employee will not take responsibility. Give them a chance to prove their ability and provide input.

5. Keep your attitude and your communication open!

CHAPTER FOUR WORKSHEET:
DIVERSITY STAFFING ASSESSMENT

1. The starting point in successful staffing in a diverse workplace is knowing how well you're currently doing. One way to do this is through the use of a formal assessment process. Considering the importance of management support, start by having all management personnel complete the Diversity Staffing Assessment provided in the Appendix for you to copy and use.

2. What problem areas or opportunities for improvement came to light from your analysis of the assessment results?

3. What specific actions do you plan to take to improve the score?

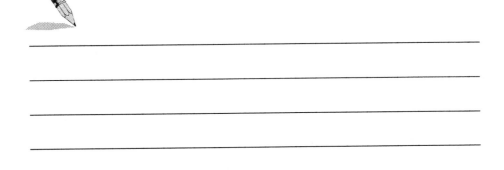

PHASE TWO: RECRUIT FOR SUCCESS

Recruiting for a highly successful diverse work force involves developing a vision for building and supporting a diverse staff within your organization. This includes recruiting both internally and externally.

Internal Recruiting

Internal recruiting usually occurs without much planning or foresight. Employees are commonly promoted into available management positions. Unfortunately, there is often a disproportionate balance of diverse workers at the front-line level versus management levels.

There are both pros and cons to internal recruiting. On one hand, promoting from within is very cost effective and can enhance morale by rewarding those who perform well. This will show others that there is a direct return on hard work. One of the downsides of internal recruiting is that your organization can miss the opportunity to bring in fresh new talent with new perspectives. Another downside of internal recruiting is that your organization can take on the qualities of being *"inbred."* An inbred organization may approach problem solving with tunnel vision, and new ideas or innovations may encounter undue resistance.

The philosophy of the Diversity Staffing Model approach is to create an atmosphere and an attitude that will encourage the advancement of individuals who might usually self-select out of the process due to environmental factors.

Consider the following components when building an internal recruiting program.

Promotions: Develop professional and leadership development programs to help candidates polish their skills. Keep in mind that more often than not, there is a disproportionate balance of diverse workers at the front line in comparison to management levels. Put support systems in place, don't assume the candidate is fine once they are promoted, they still need to be supported.

Transfers: *"Job shadowing"* opportunities can enhance learning and impact career choices. Keep in mind however, that the target environment can be either friendly or hostile. It is important to assess the *"climate"* that a new person is entering. Training may be needed to educate the potential co-workers about diversity issues before a transfer occurs.

Work Teams: Keep in mind the balance of diversity. Open communication is essential for success. Incorporate team-building activities that value the differences of all participants.

Committees: Analyze who is usually in leader and facilitator roles. Is there the potential for rotating these roles? Again, consider the balance of diversity on your committees.

Project Groups: It is important to value the input of all participants. Incorporate team-building activities that enhance communication within a diverse environment.

Always keep in mind the balance and make-up of each work group or setting. Strive for diversity at all levels to maintain the integrity of your commitment to diversity.

Once Theme Park USA . . .

had established their commitment to capitalize on diversity, they worked with Rochelle to develop a specific recruiting plan to increase the diversity of the work force.

They evaluated internal staffing practices, and realized that the organizational processes in place were very effective. The area that needed attention was getting the *"buy in"* for a renewed commitment to diversity from existing department managers. Rochelle called a meeting of all hiring managers. She enlisted Mike's help to facilitate a few diversity awareness activities.

At the meeting, Shane presented the *"Diversity Initiatives"* and shared his personal commitment to realizing those goals. Rochelle identified the following opportunities for improving the balance of diversity throughout all levels of the organization: promotions, transfers, work teams, committees, and project groups. There was much discussion about these new initiatives. Some managers were uneasy and fearful about how they would be affected, others embraced the commitment to diversity and vowed to support it completely, while the majority were somewhere in between these extremes....

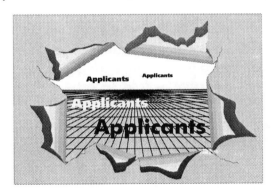

External Recruiting

External recruiting is often well-organized, having a systematic and consistent approach. Many organizations use the same resources to draw new employees year after year. The unspoken belief may be *"if it's not broken, why fix it?"* The flaw in this type of thinking is that if you don't seek out new resources, you will not diversify your applicant pool. The challenge here is to expand your horizons and seek out additional and perhaps unusual sources of applicants.

As with internal recruiting, there are both pros and cons to external recruiting. If your organization is actively seeking a skill set that is not available internally, it is to your benefit to look outside. Also, if you are seeking to improve diversity within your organization, there is a larger pool outside. However, keep in mind that there are consequences involved. Employees who do not get offered promotional opportunities are left wondering, *"Why not me?"* They may not see the skill and qualification differences being brought in from the outside. Loss of morale, loyalty and satisfaction can be potential outcomes.

Consider the following resources to increase your outreach to other applicant pools.

Personal & Professional Networking: Many opportunities to network are right at your fingertips, such as: Chamber of Commerce mixers, sporting events, school and church activities.

Community Organizations: Fundraisers are often a gathering place for people with a special interest in a particular issue. Non-profit organizations are often looking for contacts in the community. Offer to be a guest speaker for one of their meetings.

Friends & Family:
Referrals from employees can be an invaluable resource. To increase referrals, develop an incentive program to reward those employees whose referrals are hired. Next, follow up with an additional incentive for those who remain for a period of time, such as six months.

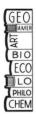

Colleges and Universities: Most colleges and universities hold Career Days, organized by campus career centers. Additionally, you can connect with specific student organizations or offices that provide services to special populations, such as Disabled Student Services.

Professional Associations: There are hundreds of organizations with a diverse membership base. Build relationships with these organizations by supporting your staff as members of particular organizations, through corporate sponsorships and by posting available positions on their job hotlines.

Service Providers: Many community-based organizations provide direct service to various populations, such as people with disabilities. These organizations often provide job placement assistance and would welcome direct contact with employers.

Building on the advertising campaign. . .
the Marketing Department had been working on, Rochelle suggested that a portion of the advertising campaign focus on increasing public awareness of the commitment to hire and support a more diverse work force.

In preparation for the upcoming summer season, Rochelle completed the Diversity Recruitment Strategies worksheet. She identified a variety of community service agencies to partner with to reach potential applicants. Rochelle developed relationships with these agencies to maintain an ongoing flow of viable candidates. Also, in response to the need for improved customer service, an effort was made to recruit people who could speak more than one language.

In addition to community organizations, Rochelle and her staff worked individually to increase their personal and professional networking, at local colleges and universities, and at various professional associations. Finally, the friends and family incentive program, *"Pick a Winner,"* continued to develop and grow. The response had been better than expected. It seemed to be one of the best resources to draw in a diverse and motivated pool of applicants.

CHAPTER FIVE WORKSHEET:
DIVERSITY RECRUITMENT STRATEGIES

Internal Recruiting

1. Identify which departments or programs are effective in supporting diversity. What are they doing well?

_____

_____

_____

_____

_____

_____

_____

2. How effective is your organization at promoting people with differences?

_____

_____

_____

_____

_____

_____

3. Who in the organization has hidden potential?
Can they be given additional training or leadership development opportunities?

_____

_____

_____

_____

_____

_____

4. What work teams, committees or project groups are currently in
place? How is the balance of diversity among the teams? What
can you do to improve the balance of diversity?

_____

_____

_____

_____

_____

_____

External Recruiting

5. Identify potential contacts and/or organizations within your area to establish a recruiting relationship.

    a. Population: Ethnicity/Race
        Contact: Community Organizations
        Who's local?

_____

_____

_____

_____

_____

_____

    b. Population: People with disabilities
        Contact: Schools/Universities/Service Providers
        Who's local?

_____

_____

_____

_____

_____

_____

c.　Population:　Retirees
　　Contact:　　Senior clubs/organizations
　　Who's local?

_____

_____

_____

_____

d.　Population:　Gay/Lesbian
　　Contact:　　Support/Community Groups
　　Who's local?

_____

_____

_____

_____

e.　Population:　Religious
　　Contact:　　Churches/Synagogues
　　Who's local?

_____

_____

_____

_____

PHASE THREE: SELECT THE BEST

Selection is the process of identifying, interviewing and selecting the most suitable candidate for an available position. This does not necessarily mean that the position is being recruited for and filled from the outside. *"Position"* here can also be defined as an opening on a committee, work team, project group, etc.

An organization that emphasizes diversity needs to include a comprehensive interview and selection process. Accurate job descriptions play an important role, as do structured and consistent interviewing techniques.

Job Analysis

In order to develop accurate job descriptions and structured interviewing techniques, you must first complete an analysis of each position within your organization. The Job Analysis Guidelines that follow will help you to complete this task.

JOB ANALYSIS GUIDELINES

Evaluate the regular duties for each position in your work group. Once you have identified the duties, break them down by the sequence of job steps. Consider the skills and competencies required to perform these steps. Always keep in mind the potential hazards and safety procedures for the job.

Analyze the specific criteria for the job:

Technical skills—Tasks such as:

- Specific knowledge relating to the job. This can range from culinary expertise for a chef, to computer expertise for a programmer.

- Physical requirements: how much lifting & how often?

- Clerical: what typing speed and what quantity/computer skills?

Performance skills such as:

- Organization: Time management ability and organizational procedures.

- Leadership: Motivation of others, able to prioritize and delegate.

- Quality: Awareness of quality customer service and products.

- Flexibility: Adaptability to change, willingness to adapt routines.

- Judgment: Problem-solving and decision-making skills.

- Initiative: Willingness to accept responsibility and take action.

- Attention to Detail: Tendency toward accuracy and clarity.

- Teamwork: Ability to contribute in a team environment.

- Communication: Language skills, both oral and auditory.

- Customer Service: Verbal communication and conflict resolution.

Other: _____

Mike was struggling...

with a job requirement to have a driver's license as an Operations Supervisor. Typically, a supervisor was not required to drive a vehicle, yet the requirement remained as a job qualification. The process of job analysis helped him identify the amount of driving required, how often, and if driving was essential. It was determined that a person was needed to make a delivery every other week. If necessary, there could be a slight change to this requirement in order to accommodate a person who could not drive....

Once the job analysis is complete, you can then develop a comprehensive written job description suitable for publication.

Jose prepared copies...

of the Job Analysis Guidelines and Targeted Interviewing Questions for the management team meeting. He and Rochelle would be teaching the hiring managers how to complete a job analysis. Rochelle said, *"The key point that I want them to hear is that our interviewing process will be consistent and unbiased, and the best way to ensure this is if we develop specific and measurable selection criteria for our opportunities at the Park."...*

Developing Interview Questions

Interviews are often stressful because you have only a short time to collect information and impressions that will enable you to make important choices that will affect the quality, productivity, and profitability of your organization. Therefore, time cannot be wasted with random, *"shoot-from-the-hip"* questions and idle chit-chat!

Once you have looked at the essential functions, skills and behaviors expected on the job, you can develop targeted interview questions. This format of questioning will help you identify and uncover the applicant's skills in each of the functional areas.

In the spaces provided on the *Job Analysis And "Targeted" Interviewing Question Worksheet,* fill in the following information:

① Identify a position you currently have open *(or, anticipate to have open in the near future).*

② Identify the two or three crucial functions of this position.

③ Choose the three critical primary responsibilities for each of the functions of this open position.

④ Describe the two or three important behavioral skills and/or knowledge and abilities required for each of these primary responsibilities. These are your selection criteria.

⑤ Develop three statements that summarize the skills, knowledge, and abilities of the position. These statements can then be combined for use in the actual job description.

⑥ For each trait/skill, develop two questions that are *"targeted"* to surface answers to assist you in evaluating candidates. Refer to the following pages of *"targeted"* interview questions for help.

The receptionist example on the following page uses the five-step process for developing *"targeted"* interview questions.

One of the key considerations of an effective interviewing and selection process is consistency. A complete job analysis and accurate job description detailing the essential functions of the job will be a solid foundation on which to build your interview. In addition, keep in mind that the process you develop needs to be utilized consistently for each applicant being interviewed.

Job Analysis And "Targeted" Interviewing Question Worksheet

① DETERMINE OPEN POSITION	② IDENTIFY FUNCTIONS	③ IDENTIFY RESPONSIBILITIES	④ IDENTIFY SKILLS, KNOWLEDGE AND ABILITIES (SELECTION CRITERIA)	⑤ DEVELOP SPECIFIC JOB DESCRIPTION	⑥ CREATE "TARGETED" INTERVIEW QUESTIONS
Receptionist	I. Manage visitors	A. Courteously greet visitors	1. Maintain professional bearing	Ability to maintain professionalism while working with both vendors and guests.	☞ "How did you handle the very persistent 'walk-in' salesperson in your last job?" ☞ (Etc.)
			2. Sincere enthusiasm for customer relations	Skilled in providing positive and enthusiastic customer relations.	☞ "What kind of people do you find most difficult to work with?" ☞ (Etc.)
			3. Strong active listening skills	Experienced with active listening techniques.	☞ "Based on what we've shared so far, why are you interested in this job?" ☞ (Etc.)
		B. Solicit reasons for visiting	1.		☞ ☞
			2.		☞ ☞
			3.		☞ ☞
		C. Direct visitors	1.		☞ ☞
			2.		☞ ☞
			3.		☞ ☞
	II. Answer phones	(Etc.)	(Etc.)		☞ (Etc.) ☞
	III. Light typing	(Etc.)	(Etc.)		☞ (Etc.) ☞

"Targeted" interview questions

Following is a representative list of *"targeted"* interview questions. Some questions may provide information about essential traits or skills in areas other than the trait/skill area in which they're listed.

Handling Responsibility

1. For what tasks in your previous job did you have full responsibility?

2. Describe a time when you were criticized for the way you handled a job.

3. What are some of the problems you encounter when doing your job, and how do you handle them?

4. How do you manage to meet your obligations in your absence (*e.g., planned vacations, off-site commitments, etc., and unplanned illnesses, etc.*)?

Working In A Diverse Group

1. What types of challenges have you experienced because of the diverse nature of a group you worked in?

2. What have you found to be the most effective way of handling these challenges?

3. What methods have you used, or observed, to handle these challenges that you would avoid using in the future? Why?

4. What are the major benefits of diversity in a work group and what have you done to bring these to the forefront?

Organizational Skills

1. How do you start a typical work day?

2. What is your procedure for meeting deadlines?

3. What have you done when you've found yourself *"swamped"*?

4. What timesaving ideas have you come up with in the past?

Communication Skills

1. What is it about yourself that makes you effective when you are speaking before a group of people?

2. What have you found to be the most effective way of communicating an idea, and persuasively explaining your point of view to your peers? To your boss?

3. What difficulties have you encountered communicating with people different from yourself?

Interpersonal Relations

1. How would you describe your relationship with your past boss? What were the greatest strengths of your boss? Weaknesses?

2. How do you feel about the way you or others in your last department were treated by your management team?

3. How do you feel your past manager evaluated your job performance? What evidence do you have to support this conclusion?

4. What kind of people do you like to work with? Which do you find most difficult to work with?

5. What have you done in the past when you've had to work closely with someone with whom you've disagreed, or had a personality conflict?

6. What have you done when someone has voiced opinions that differ from yours, especially when it's something you feel strongly about?

7. What do you expect your past employers to say when we call for references, and why?

8. If we were to call your past employer, what would he/she tell us about how you worked with others?

9. Tell me about a typical customer service problem at your last company. How did you handle it? What was the company's policy?

10. Tell me about your greatest challenge in relating to people different from yourself. Describe a situation, how you handled it, and what was the outcome?

Leadership Skills

1. What techniques have you used in your work to get others, either colleagues or employees who report to you, enthusiastic about your projects?

2. How have you delegated responsibility to others?

3. How do you meet your deadlines when people who don't report to you are called upon to deliver your work?

4. What motivates you to do a good job?

5. What strategies have you found to be helpful when managing a diverse work team?

Career Interests

1. What is your overall career objective? What have you done or plan to do to assist you in reaching this objective?

2. How do you envision your career in two years? In five years? In ten years?

3. What do you feel has contributed most to the successes *(or failures)* you've experienced in your career?

4. What are you looking for in this job that you didn't find in your past job?

5. How do you feel about the progress you have made with your present/ last company, and why?

6. Do you consider your progress on your last job representative of your ability, and why?

7. What are some of the things in a job that are important to you, and why?

8. What are some of the things you would like to avoid in a job, and why?

9. What are some of the things that motivate you in a job?

10. What disappointments *(i.e., failures, challenges, etc.)* have you found beneficial in your development? Why?

Flexibility

1. What happened when you were suddenly asked to fill in for someone else at work?

2. What do you normally do when your routine is disrupted?

3. How have you responded when you encountered unforeseen obstacles in a project you were working on?

4. How many hours should a person devote to his or her job?

5. What have you done when others (*e.g., your boss*) have resisted your ideas/recommendations?

6. How do you deal with situations in which you do not fare favorably?

7. How do you handle people who have difficulty being flexible?

Judgment

1. What have you done when you've been confronted by a problem that seemed to demand your manager's attention, and he or she was not available?

2. How do you decide on whom to ask for advice?

3. Why have you decided to leave your present job? (*Always seek more than one reason for a voluntary resignation.*)

4. Why are you interested in this job?

5. What would you say was the most, or least promising job you ever had, and what are your reasons for feeling this way?

6. How would you rank your last job against other jobs you have held, and why?

7. How do you react to rumors on the job?

8. What would you change in your current/last working environment?

Initiative

1. How have your responsibilities grown since you started your present job?

2. What new procedures or improvements did you bring to your last job?

3. What goals have you set for yourself that you've achieved?

4. If you were chosen for this job, how would you want us to assist you in your work?

Detail Orientation

1. What did you do when your work was returned to you for correction?

2. How did you maintain accuracy during periods of frequent interruptions?

3. What aspects of your previous job demanded specific attention to detail?

Teamwork

1. Describe a project you worked on as a member of a team in your last job.

2. What was your contribution?

3. Describe what you would do to make that team and that project more successful today.

4. What are your particular strengths as a team member?

5. What are your particular weaknesses as a team member?

6. What would your teammates say about you?

Don't forget that people of differing backgrounds will provide varying answers to these questions, based on different perceptions, expectations, and values such as:

♦ Views of authority *(from "unquestioning respect" to "willingness to challenge")*

♦ Individual versus group orientation *(from "individual comes first" to "the group is first and foremost")*

♦ Directness in communication *(from "the facts and nothing but" to "subtlety and face-saving")*

Now let's take a look at screening the applicants to decide who you will interview.

The Screening Process

The next step before the actual interview is the screening of applicants. Now that you have identified the selection criteria for the position, you can identify the applicants that best fit the profile you are seeking.

Look back at your *Job Analysis And "Targeted" Interviewing Question Worksheet,* and other questions you selected from the lists on preceding pages. This is the foundation for developing a screening worksheet for the individual who will be greeting the applicants. A screening sheet can be as simple as a checklist of specific and measurable qualifications, which Human Resources can use as a tool when working with the incoming applicants.

Building a diverse work force also means taking into consideration the unique perspectives of each viable candidate. Look at what a person can bring to your group. Not only will they bring the skill set you have targeted for screening, but they may also bring a different approach to problem solving, or they may bring creativity not currently represented in your technical team. Be open to all new perspectives, and guard yourself from letting your biases block clear vision.

The Interviewing Process

Here are the essential steps of the interview process and the approximate time devoted to each step.

I. Prepare (30%)
 a. Gather all relevant materials
 b. Develop list of questions
 c. Review application/resume
 d. Organize procedure
 e. Reserve meeting room

II. Establish Rapport (3%)
 a. Greet applicant positively
 b. Provide a comfortable place to sit
 c. Initiate informal conversation
 d. Respond in pleasant & courteous manner
 e. Create a relaxed & supportive atmosphere
 f. Be aware of your body language

III. Gather Information (35%)
 a. Explain the interview process
 b. Obtain essential facts & dates for future reference
 c. Take notes if necessary
 d. Use *"targeted"* interview questions
 e. Provide further information
 f. Actively listen
 g. Get a clear picture of what the applicant wants from the job

IV. Provide Information (10%)
 a. *"Sell"* the virtues of working for your organization
 b. Share an honest description of the job responsibilities
 c. Describe the position in relation to the other departments' functions
 d. Provide further information on the company *"culture,"* job expectations, policies, etc.
 e. Solicit questions from the applicant

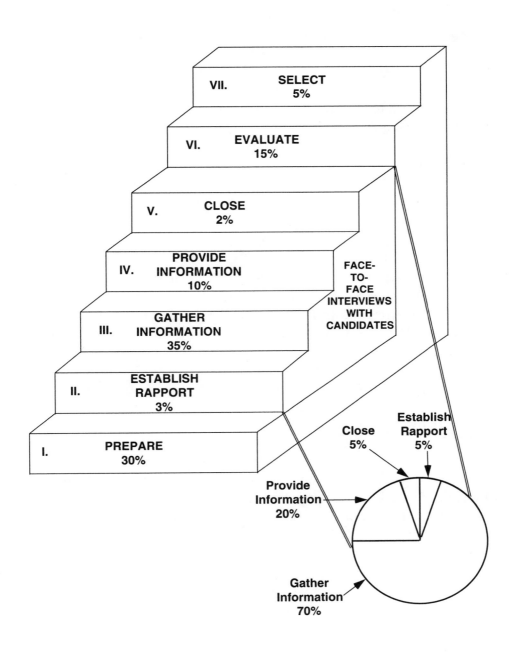

V. Close (2%)
>   a. Clearly summarize the key issues
>   b. Explain what will happen next
>   c. If desirable, provide a means for the applicant to call
>   d. Thank the applicant for his or her time & interest

VI. Evaluate (15%)
>   a. Make notes
>   b. Evaluate the facts & make judgment
>   c. Make a decision

VII. Select (5%)
>   a. Work with Human Resources to ensure a reference check
>   b. Discuss your findings with others involved
>   c. Work with Human Resources to prepare & extend an offer
>   d. Close out the process with unselected candidates

When interviewing a diverse group of applicants, be sure to assess your own biases and stereotypes that you bring to the interviewing table.   In addition, be careful of the assumptions you make about an individual with a disability and his or her ability to perform the essential functions of the job. Strive to focus on the person's ability regarding the essential functions. Provide them with ample opportunity to explain to you his or her ability to perform the job.

Evaluation

The final steps in the interviewing process are the evaluation and selection of the candidate. It is best to create a weighted rating sheet in order to be consistent and fair with applicant evaluations. It is possible to develop this rating sheet to be used as your interview form. Incorporate the interview questions with the five-point evaluation.

Let's take a look . . .
at what Theme Park USA developed to interview applicants to the Food Services Department:

INTERVIEW FORM/RATING SHEET

1. Please introduce yourself and tell me why you applied to Theme Park USA.
   (Criteria—Communication, Presentation)

Notes:_____

Rating: 1   2   3   4   5

2. Give me an example of a time when you acted as a team player. What was your role on the team? *(Criteria—Team Player)*

Notes:_____

Rating: 1   2   3   4   5

3. Tell me about an accomplishment you have made in your life that you are most proud of. *(Criteria—Initiative)*

Notes:_____

Rating: 1   2   3   4   5

4. In the business environment, things do not always go as planned, tell me about a time in your life when things did not go as planned, and how did you handle it? *(Criteria—Problem Solving)*

Notes:_____

Rating: 1   2   3   4   5

5. Tell me about a time you felt overwhelmed with responsibility and stressed. How did you handle the situation? How did you organize your time? *(Criteria—Stress, Coping)*

Notes:_____

Rating: 1   2   3   4   5

Each interviewer completes this form and takes the time to evaluate the applicant *(1 = lowest, and 5 = highest)*. Only those applicants scoring 19 points or above were offered a position with the organization.

Interviewing Pointers And Tips

Intercultural communication

Cultural communication differences stem from a basic difference in values. These values influence everything we do, and therefore can affect the most simple interactions. A job interview is anything but a simple interaction!

Let's take a look at your average interview scenario. You greet the applicant with a smile, firm handshake and eye contact as you say something like, *"It's nice to meet you Joe, come on back to my office."* As you walk to the office and begin the interview, there may be some small talk along the way about the weather, sports or whatever.

In these *"simple"* interactions before the interview, there is a lot of opportunity to set the interview off on the wrong foot. Many cultures view the handshake, eye contact, smiling and even discussion of the weather much differently. When interacting with someone from a different culture, it would be safer to tone down your approach. A more formal and professional approach is likely to be less offensive.

Rochelle met Twan . . .

in the waiting area. He was dressed nicely and had his resume with him. His qualifications were the best that Rochelle had seen all day. She was looking forward to a good interview with the hope of finally filling the accounting position. She introduced herself and extended her hand. She noticed that his grasp was very gentle and he avoided direct eye contact.

Once the interview began, it was apparent to Rochelle that Twan was either very nervous, or he was not confident about his qualifications for the job. It was a letdown and frustration for Rochelle, as she had hoped that Twan would be the one.

Just as she was winding up the interview, she remembered something from the diversity training program she attended. She recalled that it is often important to allow the applicant to discuss how others would describe their work versus describing themselves....

Additionally, she remembered that when interviewing for a technical position, it is essential for the applicant to have the opportunity to prove his or her professional and technical competence.

The next questions in Twan's interview were technically based, and he communicated very well about his ability. He convinced Rochelle that he was qualified and that he would perform the job well....

The most important attributes in developing rapport and open communication are your behavior and tone. Keep in mind that people in general do notice when they are treated with dignity and respect.

Disability issues and etiquette

Regardless of cultural background, the presence of a disability in an applicant can confound any interview scenario. The comfort (or discomfort) level of the interviewer is usually obvious to the applicant with a disability. The situation can be confusing and intimidating, for both individuals. The key concept to remember as an interviewer is that you should always accept the person as a viable candidate for the position, and discuss the applicant's ability to perform essential functions of the job.

The Human Resources Assistant, Jose . . .

was scheduled to interview applicants to fill one of the many openings in the Food Services Department. His 1:00 P.M. appointment had been with Maria. Maria had the required experience for the position and interviewed very well. Theme Park USA usually hired on the spot, and Jose was already convinced early in the interview that she was the ideal candidate. However, once he finished discussing the essential functions of the job, Maria informed Jose that she had a functional limitation due to a hidden degenerative disability.

Her limitations were that she could not walk or stand on her feet for any extended length of time. This concerned Jose, but he discussed it with one of the restaurant managers and they informed him that they could accommodate Maria by simply have a tall stool available in the cashier booth and kitchen prep areas. Maria was hired and performed well all season long!

Many interviewers believe that they need to be careful about what they say and do when interviewing a person with a disability. For example, they think they cannot use the word *"walk"* when talking with a person in a wheelchair, or that they cannot use words such as *"see"* or *"vision"* with someone who is blind. In this situation, the fear of offending the applicant can become the main concern, rather than effectively interviewing them for the job. This scenario causes stress to both parties involved. Keep in mind that the applicant is a *"person"* who happens to have a disability.

Regardless of what terminology is politically correct at the present time, it is always acceptable to call someone by their name versus label them by their disability. Also keep in mind that the person is usually not uncomfortable with their disability so you need not be uncomfortable either! The last thing this applicant wants is for you to walk on eggshells because of their apparent disability. Be yourself, and use whatever words you would naturally use in the course of an interview. Don't be trapped by the assumption that you must edit all disability related words that you think might offend them.

Additional etiquette tips

The population of people with disabilities is very large. Much of the attention focuses on people with obvious physical disabilities; however, there are many types of hidden disabilities you may encounter in the workplace. They could be anything from learning disabilities, seizure disorders, to psychological or emotional issues, diabetes, cancer, multiple sclerosis, and traumatic brain injuries.

When it comes to etiquette however, the concerns do concentrate on interacting with people who have obvious physical disabilities. The following tips will educate and help you to develop your comfort zone.

 **Handshake**—Some disabilities prevent a person from shaking hands, and others simply impair their ability to do so. Don't hesitate to extend your hand to greet an applicant who is in a wheelchair, or who may wear a brace or prosthesis, or who may have motor coordination difficulties. The handshake can act as an affirmation of the person, and avoiding it can send a negative message communicating discomfort and fear.

Eye Contact—Do not avoid eye contact to appear not to notice a disability, this will most likely backfire on you. Treat the individual as you would any other applicant. Keep in mind also that it is important to maintain eye contact with a person who is blind or visually impaired, as your voice will follow the direction you're facing.

 Verbal Communication—When interviewing a person with a speech impediment, it is essential that you understand each other. If you do not understand what is being said, ask the person to repeat what was said, or ask them to clarify. You may repeat what you understand and again ask for clarification. Never pretend to understand! If communication is that difficult, you can use pencil and paper as a means of communication.

 **Interpreters**—Sometimes a person will be accompanied by an interpreter or assistant. Always remember that it is the applicant you are interviewing, not the interpreter or assistant. Address the applicant directly.

Offering Assistance—There is a myth that people with disabilities always need help from others. This is not necessarily true. Don't assume that every person with a physical disability needs the door to be opened for them. They have probably encountered many doors before reaching your office. If an applicant, with or without a disability, drops his portfolio on the floor, it is common decency to offer to pick it up. If the applicant denies your assistance, then do not force it on them. Treat every applicant with dignity and respect and you will do well.

If you are ever in doubt about what is appropriate in a particular situation, do not hesitate to ask. It shows an awareness and sensitivity to the issues at hand. As with all communication, culturally or disability related, keep in mind that there is no one right answer. What appeals to one individual may offend another, so the general rule of thumb should be, *"When in doubt always ask the individual!"*

CHAPTER SIX WORKSHEET:
LOOKING AT YOUR SELECTION PROCESS

1. What is there about your current selection process that helps your work group/organization capitalize on diversity?

_____

_____

_____

_____

_____

_____

_____

2. What improvements could be made to your selection process to help capitalize on diversity?

    a. In the interview preparation process?

_____

_____

_____

_____

_____

b. In the screening process?

_____

_____

_____

_____

c. In the interview itself?

_____

_____

_____

_____

d. In the evaluation and selection processes?

_____

_____

_____

_____

3. For your next open position *(whether for a job opening, or a position on a team or committee)* use the *Job Analysis And "Targeted" Interviewing Question Worksheet. (Blank forms are provided in the Appendix for you to copy and use.)*

PHASE FOUR: ORIENT AND TRAIN YOUR TEAM

It is often said, *"First impressions are lasting impressions."* If your organization starts off on the wrong foot with new employees, you may never be able to regain solid footing. A new employee orientation program is the most effective means of making sure that new employees get the best possible first impression.

The aim of orientation and training is to help new employees make a smooth, positive adjustment to the workplace. It should also provide an opportunity to learn the organizational norms and values for diversity. To do this you will need a well-planned and executed orientation program that will:

- ◆ Reduce the employee's anxiety level
- ◆ Foster a positive attitude toward the organization
- ◆ Reinforce or establish realistic job expectations
- ◆ Communicate how diversity is incorporated into the norms and values of the organization, along with examples
- ◆ Communicate how diversity ties into the organization's overall vision and goals

If your organization or work group is focusing on building strength through diversity, then another set of goals enter the picture as well. In addition to covering the *"standard"* orientation goals listed above, you need to make sure new employees get a clear picture of the philosophy and approach to diversity.

Specific diversity-related points to cover in the orientation include:

♦ Communicating how diversity ties into the organization's overall vision and goals.

♦ Providing specific examples of how diversity has played a role in achieving these goals.

♦ Communicating how diversity is incorporated into the norms and values of the organization, along with examples.

♦ Providing information on specific training, tools, techniques, and other opportunities for new employees to develop specific skills needed in a diverse workplace.

♦ Providing an assessment tool or process so new employees can have a gauge of how their own expectations, values, and perceptions influence their approach to working in a diverse workplace.

♦ Communicating behavioral expectations (value, support and encouragement) for interactions with all members of the diverse workplace.

Once you determine the goals of the orientation process, you are ready to select the appropriate tools and approaches to use.

The goal of orientation and training for new *(or existing)* employees is to continually improve the match between the job requirements and the skills and competencies of the employees.

There are many tools and opportunities for orientation and training within your organization such as:

- ◆ On-The-Job Training
- ◆ Job Aids
- ◆ Computer-Based Training
- ◆ Classroom Training
- ◆ Meetings *(committee, staff, team)*
- ◆ Memos & Bulletins

In order to determine your best approach to orienting and training new employees, first determine the behavioral outcomes you desire.

BEHAVIOR OUTCOME	DESCRIPTION	COMMON TRAINING METHODS
Knowledge	Internalization of information	Lecture Reading Structured Discussion
Understanding	Knowledge of how to apply information on the job	Structured Discussion Case Study Personal Action Planning
Skills	Incorporation of new on-the-job behaviors	Role Play Practice Application Personal Action Planning
Attitudes and Interests	Satisfying exposure to, and demonstration of, new on-the-job behaviors	Structured Discussion Case Study Role Play Practice Application Action Planning

Learning Styles and Differences

When dealing with the many diverse backgrounds of your new employees, it is important to consider not only differences in communication, but also differences in learning styles due to cultural or disability issues. It may be necessary to accommodate a disability within the training environment. For example, a deaf individual may need an interpreter, or a person with a learning disability may need extended training and/or testing time.

To be effective in this environment, it is essential that you remember the different modalities in which people learn.

♦ Visual: Means that a person learns more effectively through what they see.

♦ Auditory: Means that a person learns and processes information primarily through what they hear.

♦ Kinesthetic: A kinesthetic learner works more effectively by doing what it is they are trying to learn.

Truly effective training will utilize all approaches to learning to maximize the retention rate of the learner.

"Trainees learn only 16 percent of what they read; 20 percent of what they see; 30 percent of what they are told; 50 percent of what they see and are told and 70 percent of what they see, are told and respond to; and 90 percent of what they do."

Joe L. Whitley

Mike, the Training Coordinator . . .

for Park Operations, was always fascinated by the learning differences of individuals, and the impact of learning disabilities on the training process.

He had already made changes to accommodate people with disabilities within the training environment. This included ensuring that the training facility was wheelchair accessible, that employees with learning disabilities were provided extended time on tests if necessary, and that all materials were available in written form. Mike would be doing further research on other types of accommodations that might be needed during training such as: large print or braille materials, interpreters for deaf or hearing impaired individuals, tape recorded sessions and/or note takers for the visually impaired.

Mike really believed in the importance of using a variety of teaching styles to get his ideas across. He constantly evaluated his training programs to make them as active and interactive as possible, to enhance the learning process for all participants....

Effective Presentation Tips

♦ Use all modalities: Auditory, Visual, Kinesthetic

♦ Keep training active, visual, and interactive with games and activities

♦ Incorporate visual aids: flip charts, videos, overheads

♦ Create time for informal group discussion, use alternating facilitators

♦ Allow people to ask questions anonymously (in writing)

♦ Have handouts available

♦ Utilize role play scenarios to increase understanding

♦ Have an organized presentation to avoid straying

♦ Do not try to cover too much information at one time

Seven Common Training Methods

When designing on-the-job training plans, you will more than likely be concerned with, *"What is the most effective method to get the content across to employees?"* Although there are few simple answers, it is important to consider the advantages and disadvantages of each of the seven common training methods listed below, and to take into consideration potential issues relating to the diversity of your group.

Lecture

One-way verbal delivery of content by the trainer

Advantages	**Disadvantages**
➠ Can reinforce trainer's credibility and authority	➠ One-way not effective if goal is shared responsibility
➠ Information is concentrated and organized as desired	➠ Relative passivity of employees being trained
➠ Efficient; lots of information can be shared	➠ Depends totally on trainer's effectiveness and information
➠ Can be personalized/customized easily	➠ Usually no record of key points; comprehensiveness and consistency are suspect
	➠ Words and figures can easily be garbled

Potential Diversity Issues:

♦ People of some cultures and backgrounds expect to play a passive role in these settings.

♦ Others will feel more comfortable in a setting where they can *"challenge"* the trainer and ask *"tough"* questions.

♦ People who are *"visual"* learners may tune out very quickly, and will not retain the information.

Reading

Individual reading of training manuals
during a structured time frame

Advantages

⇒ Gives a complete picture; all necessary details in carefully chosen words

⇒ Exposes employees to large quantities of content in a concentrated time frame

⇒ Learners have a good chance to study content

⇒ Provides opportunity to review materials during and after the training experience

⇒ Easily passed on to other interested parties

Disadvantages

⇒ May take a lot of time to prepare

⇒ Materials are competing with other references, memos, mail, etc.

⇒ May seem tedious or boring to some employees

⇒ Can't get immediate reaction of the learner

⇒ Difficult to hold employees accountable for content; it can be forgotten or put aside

Potential Diversity Issues:

♦ People have different reading abilities due to their language capability and background.

♦ People from backgrounds that lean toward learning through personal interaction will be at a disadvantage.

♦ Some people with learning disabilities have slower or less effective visual processing and may not retain or grasp what is read.

Structured Discussion

*Structured conversations between employees
(in small or large groups), aimed toward specific learning objectives*

Advantages

➠ Can explain and demonstrate at the same time

➠ Highly personal interaction among employees, and creative idea sharing

➠ Can interrupt to ask questions and clarify points

➠ Past experiences of employees contribute to the learning process

➠ Can be guided by facial expressions

➠ Can take care of brief items as they arise

Disadvantages

➠ May be dominated by a few employees

➠ Subject to interruptions and diversions

➠ Potential creation of side discussions that don't apply

➠ Can't always remember everything to cover or appropriate words

Potential Diversity Issues:

◆ Some groups will be uncomfortable with the *"open-forum"* approach.

◆ People may need to break through the stereotypes they hold to fully participate in an interactive, diverse group setting.

◆ Some people will be uncomfortable discussing certain issues, such as management style or communication.

Case Study

Written description of situations that contain enough details so employees can discuss specific recommendations

Advantages	Disadvantages
➡ Can gain a shared understanding of on-the-job problems	➡ Difficult to develop and incorporate all the necessary details
➡ Can provide *"real-world"* applications when customized	➡ Only builds and demonstrates understanding, not skills

Potential Diversity Issues:
♦ Many prepackaged cases available in the marketplace do not reflect the nature of a diverse workplace.

Role Play

Reenactment of a specific situation by the employees who are provided with made-up role descriptions

Advantages	Disadvantages
➡ Allows for the practice of specific behaviors during on-the-job training	➡ Resistance of employees to *"play act"* with peers
➡ Skill mastery is easier to detect	➡ Key learning points may be lost in all the action if not properly facilitated
➡ Less threatening since employees are *"playing a role"* versus being themselves with others	➡ Some employees may feel that situations are not *"real-world"*

Potential Diversity Issues:
♦ Stereotypes may get in the way of effective role-play participation.
♦ Some groups may be uncomfortable with role playing certain issues, such as challenging authority.

Practice Application

Immediate skill application in a specific on-the-job situation the employees are currently facing

Advantages	Disadvantages
➠ Practice handling a *"real-world"* situation and task using specific skills from training	➠ Employees may often attempt to solve specific *"real-world"* situations being practiced rather than focus on skill development
➠ Opportunity to receive immediate coaching feedback	➠ Some learners prefer time to digest information first instead of *"diving in"* immediately

Potential Diversity Issues:

♦ Those involved in coaching and feedback need to understand any communication issues relevant to their *"partner's"* background. Comfort levels will vary.

Personal Action Planning

Identification of specific activities that employees are committed to carry out back on the job

Advantages	Disadvantages
➠ Immediate and focused application of skills, knowledge, or behaviors	➠ Some employees may be unwilling to make a commitment
➠ Facilitates the documentation and reinforcement of key learning points while still at work	➠ Plans may lack follow-up and accountability mechanisms

Potential Diversity Issues:

♦ People of certain backgrounds might appear to agree to impossible performance targets to avoid the perception of challenging authority.

♦ Some individuals are more comfortable with group goals rather than individual goals.

Developing On-The-Job Training Plans

Orientation and training should continue as new employees begin to tackle their day-to-day job responsibilities. Following is an example of a tool to help plan their on-the-job training.

Employee: Dana Mills		**Training Objectives:** Following on-the-job-training, Dana will be able to answer the phones by the second ring in a professional manner and take complete, legible, handwritten messages		
Behavioral Outcomes: Understand skills		**Training Methods:** Structured discussion, practical application, and role playing		
WHAT • training option • specific actions/topics	**WHO** • trainer • trainee(s) • evaluator	**HOW** • process • resources • required time • budget • materials • equipment • staff	**WHEN/WHERE** • schedule • location	**WHY** • reasons • benefits • expectations • measurements
1. Discuss /define importance of complete and legible messages	Janet Dana	Structured discussion interview for important internal customers	Monday	Ensure Dana understands importance of message
2. Observe Dana taking messages for 30 min. Note suggestions for improvement and review messages Provide feedback	Janet Dana	Direct and objective note taking	Monday	Provide effective feedback and coaching
3. Practice taking messages for a tough call	Janet Dana	Role play (call in)	Monday	Test new skills
4. Dana to scrutinize key learning points and methods to ensure messages are complete and legible	Janet Dana	Written summary	Tuesday	Ensure Dana has integrated learning into daily work

Orienting new employees is a key element in ensuring all employees are *"on-board"* for success through diversity.

CHAPTER SEVEN WORKSHEET:
LOOKING AT YOUR ORIENTATION PROCESS

1. In what ways does your current new employee orientation program reflect your work group's and organization's commitment to diversity?

_____

_____

_____

_____

_____

_____

2. What improvements could be made to the orientation program?

_____

_____

_____

_____

_____

_____

_____

_____

3. Given the advantages and disadvantages of the seven common training methods and the diverse make-up of your work group, what would be some of the pros and cons of each method for your group's orientation and training program?

METHOD	PROS	CONS
Lecture		
Reading		
Structured Discussion		
Case Study		
Role Play		
Practice Application		
Personal Action Planning		

PHASE FIVE: RETAIN AND MAINTAIN YOUR DIVERSITY

The key to successful staffing in a diverse workplace is in the ability to retain staff members while maintaining the focus on diversity as a *"core"* strength. Keep in mind that making a commitment to diversity means more than striving for immediate results such as improved demographics within your organization. Simply recruiting for diversity will not necessarily mean that those whom you employ will stay with your organization if they do not feel welcome or supported.

Establish Ground Rules

Diverse organizations and work groups, because of their nature, have an obligation to address diversity through specific ground rules. These rules are needed to create an environment in which people of different backgrounds can understand one another and work toward organizational goals. Consider some of the following for your own ground rules.

♦ Our organization's diversity is one of our strengths, and we need to nurture it

♦ Make communication open and honest; no interruptions permitted

♦ Recognize that people may approach problems differently; listen and consider other points of view

♦ Make provisions for a forum to discuss and resolve diversity issues, when needed

♦ Remember that off-color and demeaning jokes are unacceptable and that diverse team members are not to be insulted.

♦ Encourage new ideas

Let's put it in writing . . .

said Shane. *"Everyone needs to be clear about the ground rules for diversity in our park."*

♦ The organization will benchmark progress utilizing the Diversity Staffing Assessment.

♦ New employees will complete an orientation program on their first day, this will include information about our Diversity Initiatives.

♦ In daily communication with each other, we will all make an effort to focus on both the message and the messenger.

♦ All employees will accept responsibility for playing a role in conflict resolution.

♦ All employees will strive to respect the differences of their co-workers.

♦ Management personnel will support the Diversity Initiatives, and encourage diversity within each work setting.

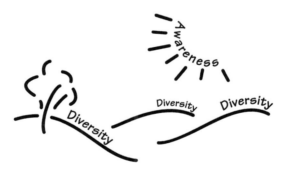

Beyond Staff Development And Awareness

Training programs geared toward heightening the awareness level and appreciation for diversity can be helpful to educate employees as your organization enforces its commitment to diversity. However, training and development can not be a stand-alone activity. There must be additional support systems in place such as:

Support groups—Nontraditional managers need a support system to survive the challenges of being a pioneer. You can hold *"brown bag"* seminars on topics of interest to employees. This may be a way to establish a regular routine.

Career development—Can your organization provide opportunities for continuous growth and personal development? Since there are fewer positions at the top of most organizations, many employees are very interested in lateral moves to provide variety and new challenges.

Job sharing—With the challenges of balancing work and family issues, many people are interested in alternative work situations such as job sharing.

Child care alternatives—Evaluate the feasibility of developing an in-house child care program. Smaller organizations can investigate the possibility of partnering with a local child care agency and then extend discounts to their employees.

Flexible work schedules—Employees with children often have very hectic schedules in the morning. Can you be flexible enough for an employee to come in later in the morning and stay later in the evening? How about evenings and weekends?

Mentoring—This is a proven way to groom future management personnel. It is a casual relationship with a new employee and an experienced employee. Mentoring is most successful when mentors act as career counselors, who at the same time advocate for their mentoree's accountability and promotability.

As a result of support systems and services in place, employees are likely to be less stressed and more satisfied with your organization. Many of these options would solve some of the difficulties of daily work life, resulting in more productive and committed employees in your organization.

Shane's goal and the vision...

of Theme Park USA was to increase the retention rate of employees. The main focus was creating an environment that would support and encourage employees from all backgrounds.

In keeping with the fun and positive atmosphere of a theme park, Shane developed an interdepartmental, competitive *"crazy sports"* event. Each department within the park selected a team of players. The only parameters for the teams were that they represent the diversity of the staff within the department.

The winning team of this event was crowned the most energetic and fun department! Incentives and prizes were awarded as well. This event served as a launching point to build camaraderie and spirit within the organization. Working together to reach a common goal was then translated into the Diversity Initiatives of the organization.

Other programs and services offered in support of diversity included discounted child care services at a local agency. Flex schedules were offered to employees who developed a working plan for alternative hours. Classes in literacy and English as a second language were offered on a volunteer basis to employees. Volunteer opportunities were created with the development of the literacy program. Theme Park USA also decided to offer a tuition assistance plan to help those individuals who wanted to further their education.

Supervising A Diverse Work Force

Excellent communication skills are not inherited, they are learned and they require constant reevaluation and revision. A manager who is aware of the issues of cross-cultural communication may need to change his or her style of communication depending on whom they are speaking with.

It is often taken for granted that clear two-way communication will occur between employee and supervisor. What is not considered however, is the difference in communication styles between culture and gender. Differences also occur with attitudes toward authority. In many cultures, for example, age is to be respected, males are often found in positions of authority, employees should not question authority, and workers do not act without direct orders from their superior.

Performance reviews can be a difficult situation for any manager. Providing feedback, both positive and negative is often uncomfortable. Add to this situation cultural differences in values, authority, and communication, and you have a potentially confusing and unclear interaction.

Strategies For Effective Communication

Here are some suggestions for providing constructive feedback:

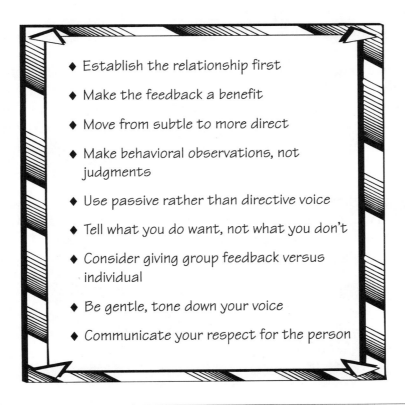

- ◆ Establish the relationship first
- ◆ Make the feedback a benefit
- ◆ Move from subtle to more direct
- ◆ Make behavioral observations, not judgments
- ◆ Use passive rather than directive voice
- ◆ Tell what you *do* want, not what you *don't*
- ◆ Consider giving group feedback versus individual
- ◆ Be gentle, tone down your voice
- ◆ Communicate your respect for the person

- **Establish the relationship first.** Feedback is often most effective and valued as relevant when it is being delivered by someone you know to be a caring and sincere individual.

- **Make the feedback a benefit.** Feedback can be positioned so as to appear to be a benefit. For example, the opportunity for improved performance can also mean a greater chance at receiving a raise.

- **Move from subtle to more direct.** In order to save face, sometimes it is advantageous to be less direct about a particular problem. For example, a supervisor could suggest that a work area be looked at again for cleanliness, and if the subtle hint is not understood, feedback can become progressively more direct.

- **Make behavioral observations, not judgments.** To decrease a defensive reaction, comment specifically on the behavior in question. Avoid making general judgmental types of statements about an individual or his or her character.

- **Use passive rather than directive voice.** Instead of using *"You"* statements such as, *"You were late!"* try this, *"The store did not open until 9:15 this morning."* Let the employee infer his or her role and responsibility.

♦ **Tell what you do want, not what you don't.** Be positive when providing information, don't make it a reprimand. For example: instead of, *"Don't be late for that meeting,"* try this, *"The meeting starts at 9:00 A.M., I'll see you there."*

♦ **Consider giving group feedback versus individual.** Some cultures emphasize the group over the individual. In this situation, providing negative feedback to the group *(even though it was an individual's situation)* would work well to create a sense of accountability through peer pressure.

♦ **Be gentle, tone down your voice.** Sometimes people don't realize the impact they make with their voices. Even though you may think your voice is fine, it can sound very loud to others. Speak softly, in a gentle tone of voice and find a quiet place to meet.

♦ **Communicate your respect for the person.** Speak with both actions and words to convey the respect you have for an individual.

Using these strategies for effective communication will be beneficial when interacting with employees on a regular basis.

CHAPTER EIGHT WORKSHEET: RETAINING AND MAINTAINING YOUR GROUP'S DIVERSITY

1. What additional ground rules should your group adopt to clarify its commitment to the group's diversity?

_____

_____

_____

_____

_____

_____

2. What support system does your work group currently have? Given the group's diverse make-up, should there be changes made?

_____

_____

_____

_____

_____

3. What kinds of issues do managers need to address *(their skills, approaches, etc.)* to better meet the needs of their diverse staff?

_____

_____

_____

_____

_____

_____

_____

_____

_____

4. Use the following check list when preparing feedback for a staff member.

- ☐ Establish the relationship first
- ☐ Make the feedback a benefit
- ☐ Move from subtle to more direct
- ☐ Make behavioral observations, not judgments
- ☐ Use passive rather than directive voice
- ☐ Tell what you do want, not what you don't
- ☐ Consider giving group feedback versus individual
- ☐ Be gentle, tone down your voice
- ☐ Communicate your respect for the person

CHAPTER NINE

SUMMARY

Building and retaining a diverse work force takes time, tolerance and patience. The benefits of diversity far outweigh the drawbacks. A diverse work force is more effective and provides improved work force quality, increased market sensitivity, and organizational flexibility.

The Diversity Staffing Model provides the structure and steps to effectively develop the diversity of your organization.

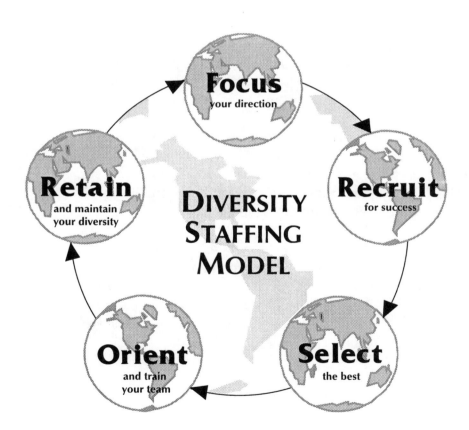

Focus: This gives you the opportunity to evaluate and identify the key values and priorities within your organization. The process takes you through the steps of goal setting, committing, communicating and empowering the initiatives of diversity in your employees.

Recruit: This provides ideas and structure for developing a successful recruiting campaign. It defines the differences between internal and external recruiting. It makes suggestions for resources to use within the community.

Select: The essential steps of the selection process are detailed. You read about the importance of structured and consistent interviewing techniques. In addition, a worksheet is provided to assist you in completing a job analysis, developing a specific job description, and targeted interviewing questions.

Orient: Effective orientation and training utilizes multiple learning methods to maximize learning. People learn through seeing, hearing and doing, and typically retain more information through actively doing what they are trying to learn.

Retain: To keep a balance of diversity within your organization, you must have the support systems in place. Career development, support groups, and brown bag seminars are just a few examples that will put you in the right direction.

Your personal and organizational commitment to diversity is the only way to begin building an effective and retained work force.

Remember that the dynamics of diversity are here to stay. A diverse workplace is inevitable, but the benefits of diversity are not. Managing these changes effectively will help you to reap the benefits. One of the most important aspects to remember here, is that specific steps must be taken to create an environment where all personnel feel welcome and valued for what they bring to your organization.

The Diversity Staffing Model will get you on the right tack toward initiating action in support of diversity. It is not an overnight process, it may take time to evoke true change in your organization. Take the first step to *"Focus"* your direction, and you will be on your way!

REPRODUCIBLE FORMS AND WORKSHEETS

The pages in the Appendix are provided for you to photocopy and use appropriately.

DIVERSITY STAFFING ASSESSMENT

Check the appropriate box using the scale where you:
(1) = Strongly disagree, (2) = Disagree, (3) = Neither agree nor disagree, (4) = Agree, (5) = Strongly agree.

		1	2	3	4	5
1.	Your organization has a stated vision/goal for diversity.					
2.	All employees understand the definition of diversity.					
3.	All accept the vision.					
4.	The organization's commitment to diversity is reflected in its staffing processes.					
5.	Applicants for new positions recognize immediately the organization's goals of capitalizing on diversity.					
6.	Your organization encourages open communication with one another.					
7.	Your department actively recruits diverse members.					
8.	The interviewing process and methodologies take into account the different values and needs of the diverse applicant group.					
9.	Your selection process has been evaluated for potential biases.					
10.	Promotional opportunities are equally available to members from diverse backgrounds.					
11.	Your department encourages individual interaction across diversity lines.					
12.	The employee orientation process reflects the organization's commitment to diversity.					
13.	Employees appreciate and respect each other's unique talents and skills.					

		1	2	3	4	5
14.	Employees can count on one another, regardless of their differences.					
15.	Employees constructively deal with interpersonal problems and conflicts.					
16.	Employees can determine whether problems are diversity related.					
17.	Work groups effectively retain and maintain their group diversity.					

Scoring Key

81 to 85—Excellent

Congratulations! Your staffing process is geared to ensuring your organization or work group capitalizes on its diversity. You should try to communicate the strengths of your group's approach to other people or teams within your organization who may not be as far along as you.

75 to 80—Very Good

Your staffing approach has all the ingredients for success. However, you may need to fine-tune areas that received lower scores. Address these areas to find out what can be done to improve them. Develop specific action plans and take the assessment again in a month or two to track your improvement.

61 to 75—Opportunity for Growth

Your group has some core strengths, but clearly there are areas for growth and improvement. Review the areas that received the lowest scores. Also look at the one or two areas that received the highest scores. Evaluate the dynamics of how these strengths were achieved—there may be clues for building the other areas.

60 or Less—Watch out! Sharp Curves!

Your organization does not appear to be ready. In fact, you may already be experiencing some problems Hopefully this assessment provides you with a starting point on which to focus. Choose one or two specific areas and plan for progress in small steps. Consider bringing in an outside facilitator to help get you started toward building diversity in your work force.

JOB ANALYSIS GUIDELINES

Evaluate the regular duties for each position in your work group. Once you have identified the duties, break them down by the sequence of job steps. Consider the skills and competencies required to perform these steps. Always keep in mind the potential hazards and safety procedures for the job.

Analyze the specific criteria for the job:

Technical skills—Tasks such as:

♦ Specific knowledge relating to the job. This can range from culinary expertise for a chef, to computer expertise for a programmer.

♦ Physical requirements: How much lifting & how often?

♦ Clerical: What typing speed and what quantity/computer skills?

Performance skills such as:

♦ Organization: Time management ability and organizational procedures.

♦ Leadership: Motivation of others, able to prioritize and delegate.

♦ Quality: Awareness of quality customer service and products.

♦ Flexibility: Adaptability to change, willingness to adapt routines.

♦ Judgement: Problem-solving and decision-making skills.

♦ Initiative: Willingness to accept responsibility and take action.

♦ Attention to Detail: Tendency toward accuracy and clarity.

♦ Teamwork: Ability to contribute in a team environment.

♦ Communication: Language skills, both oral and auditory

♦ Customer Service: Verbal communication and conflict resolution.

Other: _____

JOB ANALYSIS AND "TARGETED" INTERVIEWING QUESTION WORKSHEET

① DETERMINE OPEN POSITION	② IDENTIFY FUNCTIONS	③ IDENTIFY RESPONSIBILITIES	④ IDENTIFY SKILLS, KNOWLEDGE AND ABILITIES (SELECTION CRITERIA)	⑤ DEVELOP SPECIFIC JOB DESCRIPTION	⑥ CREATE "TARGETED" INTERVIEW QUESTIONS
	I.	A.	1.		☞ ☞
			2.		☞ ☞
			3.		☞ ☞
		B.	1.		☞ ☞
			2.		☞ ☞
			3.		☞ ☞
		C.	1.		☞ ☞
			2.		☞ ☞
			3.		☞ ☞
	II.	A.	1.		☞ ☞
			2.		☞ ☞
			3.		☞ ☞
		B.	1.		☞ ☞
			2.		☞ ☞
			3.		☞ ☞

INTERVIEW FORM/RATING SHEET

1. Please introduce yourself and tell me why you applied to Theme Park USA.
   (Criteria—Communication, Presentation)

Notes:_____

Rating: 1   2   3   4   5

2. Give me an example of a time when you acted as a team player. What was
   your role on the team? *(Criteria—Team Player)*

Notes:_____

Rating: 1   2   3   4   5

3. Tell me about an accomplishment you have made in your life that you are
   most proud of. *(Criteria—Initiative)*

Notes:_____

Rating: 1   2   3   4   5

4. In the business environment, things do not always go as planned, tell me
   about a time in your life when things did not go as planned, and how did you
   handle it? *(Criteria—Problem Solving)*

Notes:_____

Rating: 1   2   3   4   5

5. Tell me about a time you felt overwhelmed with responsibility and stressed.
   How did you handle the situation? How did you organize your time?
   (Criteria—Stress, Coping)

Notes:_____

Rating: 1   2   3   4   5

Each interviewer completes this form and takes the time to evaluate the
applicant (*1 = lowest and 5 = highest).* Only those applicants scoring 19 points
or above are offered a position with the organization.

ON-THE-JOB TRAINING PLANNER

Employee:	Training Objectives:			
Behavioral Outcomes:	Training Methods:			
WHAT	**WHO**	**HOW**	**WHEN/ WHERE**	**WHY**

SAMPLE NEW EMPLOYEE
ORIENTATION CHECKLIST

_____   _____
Name   **Start Date**

During the first three months of employment, the new employee's hiring supervisor
and/or designated department representative should cover the following items:

Check If Done:

_____ 1.   Provide essential resources and references:

    ____ Organizational marketing literature   ____ Organizational charts
    ____ Product/service promotions, etc.   ____ Job descriptions
    ____ Mission, values, philosophy, etc.   ____ HR/policy manual
    ____ Strategic plans, goals, objectives, etc.   ____ Employee handbook
    ____ Organizational and departmental procedures   ____ Key forms, checklists, etc.

_____ 2.   Review the job description and performance expectations/standards.

_____ 3.   Review the work schedule *(include lunch, breaks, overtime, time clock, etc.).*

_____ 4.   Review the payroll timing, policies, and procedures.

_____ 5.   Review key policies:

    ____ Attendance/punctuality   ____ Personal conduct standards
    ____ Sick days/leaves of absence   ____ Progressive disciplinary actions
        (e.g., whom to notify)   ____ Confidentiality
    ____ Holidays   ____ Safety/accident procedures
    ____ Vacations/scheduling procedures   ____ Health/first aid
    ____ Standard work shift   ____ Emergency procedures
    ____ Overtime   ____ Preventive maintenance
    ____ Performance appraisal   ____ Conflict of interest
    ____ Wage/salary administration   ____ Smoking/nonsmoking areas
    ____ Dress code   ____ Visitors
    ____ Office appearance   ____ Personal status changes

_____ 6.   Review general administrative procedures:

    ____ Time cards   ____ Business cards
    ____ Office/desk/work station keys   ____ ID cards/security access
    ____ Calendars/schedules   ____ Expense reports
    ____ Pertinent reports/lists   ____ General supplies

_____ 7.   Give introductions to members of immediate staff *(include brief
background of each)* and other key personnel

_____ **8.** Review standard meetings to attend:

	MEETINGS	PURPOSE	MEMBERS	TIMES
a.				
b.				
c.				

_____ **9.** Give a brief tour of the surrounding area and facilities, including:

____ Rest rooms   ____ Equipment/tools/supplies
____ Telephones/message systems   ____ Storage/files
____ Pay phones   ____ Books/references
____ Mail distribution/center   ____ Break room/kitchen
____ Copy machines/fax   ____ Coffee/vending machines
____ Bulletin boards   ____ Eating establishments
____ Appointment books/schedules   ____ Drinking fountains
____ Time clock   ____ Parking
____ Computer systems/printers   ____ Emergency exits

_____ **10.** Present initial job assignments and training plans.

	ASSIGNMENTS	TRAINING PLANS
a.		
b.		
c.		
d.		

_____ **11.** Identify co-workers (*other than the hiring supervisor*) who will train the new employee and/or act as a "buddy" to assist with general questions:

	GO TO THIS CO-WORKER	FOR TRAINING AND/OR ASSISTANCE REGARDING
a.		
b.		

_____ **12.** Plan for initial lunches (*designate someone to spend time with the new employee, such as a member of the management team, co-workers, and/or other employees during the first few days/weeks*).

_____ **13.** Other: _____

_____ _____ _____ _____
Hiring Supervisor's Signature   Date   New Employee's Signature   Date

THE PRACTICAL GUIDEBOOK COLLECTION FROM RICHARD CHANG ASSOCIATES, INC. PUBLICATIONS DIVISION

Our Practical Guidebook Collection is growing to meet the challenges of the ever-changing workplace of the 90's. Available through Richard Chang Associates, Inc., fine bookstores, training and organizational development resource catalogs and distributed internationally.

QUALITY IMPROVEMENT SERIES

- Meetings That Work!
- Continuous Improvement Tools Volume 1
- Continuous Improvement Tools Volume 2
- Step-By-Step Problem Solving
- Satisfying Internal Customers First!
- Continuous Process Improvement
- Improving Through Benchmarking
- Succeeding As A Self-Managed Team
- Process Reengineering In Action
- Measuring Organizational Improvement Impact

MANAGEMENT SKILLS SERIES

- Coaching Through Effective Feedback
- Expanding Leadership Impact
- Mastering Change Management
- On-The-Job Orientation And Training
- Re-Creating Teams During Transitions

HIGH PERFORMANCE TEAM SERIES

- Success Through Teamwork
- Team Decision-Making Techniques
- Measuring Team Performance
- Building A Dynamic Team

HIGH-IMPACT TRAINING SERIES

- Creating High-Impact Training
- Identifying Targeted Training Needs
- Mapping A Winning Training Approach
- Producing High-Impact Learning Tools
- Applying Successful Training Techniques
- Measuring The Impact Of Training
- Make Your Training Results Last

WORKPLACE DIVERSITY SERIES

- Capitalizing On Workplace Diversity
- Successful Staffing In A Diverse Workplace
- Team Building For Diverse Work Groups
- Communicating In A Diverse Workplace
- Tools For Valuing Diversity

ADDITIONAL RESOURCES
FROM RICHARD CHANG ASSOCIATES, INC.

Improve your training sessions and seminars with the ideal tools—videos from Richard Chang Associates, Inc. You and your team will easily relate to the portrayals of real-life workplace situations. You can apply our innovative techniques to your own situations for immediate results.

TRAINING VIDEOTAPES

Mastering Change Management*
Turning Obstacles Into Opportunities

Step-By-Step Problem Solving*
A Practical Approach To Solving Problems On The Job

Quality: You Don't Have To Be Sick To Get Better**
Individuals Do Make a Difference

Achieving Results Through Quality Improvement**

*Authored by Dr. Richard Chang and produced by Double Vision Studios.
**Produced by American Media Inc. in conjunction with Richard Chang Associates, Inc.
  Each video includes a Facilitator's Guide.

"THE HUMAN EDGE SERIES" VIDEOTAPES

Total Quality: Myths, Methods, Or Miracles
Featuring Drs. Ken Blanchard and Richard Chang

Empowering The Quality Effort
Featuring Drs. Ken Blanchard and Richard Chang

Produced by Double Vision Studios.

"THE TOTAL QUALITY SERIES"
TRAINING VIDEOTAPES AND WORKBOOKS

Building Commitment *(Telly Award Winner)*
How To Build Greater Commitment To Your TQ Efforts

Teaming Up
How To Successfully Participate On Quality-Improvement Teams

Applied Problem Solving
How To Solve Problems As An Individual Or On A Team

Self-Directed Evaluation
How To Establish Feedback Methods To Self-Monitor Improvements

Authored by Dr. Richard Chang and produced by Double Vision Studios, each videotape from *"The Total Quality Series"* includes a *Facilitator's Guide* and five *Participant Workbooks* with each purchase. Additional *Participant Workbooks* are available for purchase.

EVALUATION AND FEEDBACK FORM

We need your help to continuously improve the quality of the resources provided through the Richard Chang Associates, Inc., Publications Division. We would greatly appreciate your input and suggestions regarding this particular guidebook, as well as future guidebook interests.

Please photocopy this form before completing it, since other readers may use this guidebook. Thank you in advance for your feedback.

Guidebook Title: _____

1. Overall, how would you rate your *level of satisfaction* with this guidebook? Please circle your response.

    Extremely Dissatisfied   Satisfied   Extremely Satisfied

    1   2   3   4   5

2. What specific *concepts or methods* did you find <u>most</u> helpful?

    _____

    _____

3. What specific *concepts or methods* did you find <u>least</u> helpful?

    _____

    _____

4. As an individual who may purchase additional guidebooks in the future, what *characteristics/features/benefits* are most important to you in making a decision to purchase a guidebook *(or another similar book)*?

    _____

    _____

5. What additional *subject matter/topic areas* would you like to see addressed in future guidebooks?

    _____

    _____

Name *(optional):*_____

Address: _____

C/S/Z: _____   **Phone (   )** _____

PLEASE FAX YOUR RESPONSES TO: (714) 756-0853
OR CALL US AT: 1-800-756-8096